Sophie

Sophie

Edward "Skip" Biron

To order additional copies of this book, contact:
Xlibris
1-888-795-4274
www.Xlibris.com
Orders@Xlibris.com
746978

Contents

Dedication

I wish to dedicate this book to pet lovers everywhere who consider their pet as a very special member of the family.

Chapter 1

Introduction

Everyone has heard the expression, "A dog is man's best friend." For thousands of years, dogs have worked to earn this distinction. They have provided not only love and affection, but have worked side-by-side with people in every aspect of the human condition. Studies have been conducted to prove the physical, emotional and social benefits of owning a dog. Canine companionship has been given credit for improving the quality of people's lives in many ways; such as, by increasing longevity, reducing blood pressure, cholesterol and triglycerides, reducing depression, stress, anxiety and loneliness as well as keeping them active.

The first reference to that phrase was supposedly in 1789 by Frederick II, King of Prussia at a time when people began to exhibit emotional and tender feelings for their dogs and they were thought to possess a tremendous sense of loyalty to their masters. The term was very likely popularized by a poem written by Ogden Nash in 1949, "An Introduction to Dogs." The first line of that poem is: "A dog is man's best friend."

Dogs are awesome companions. No matter where they are or what they are doing, they always seem to save the day. Dogs save people from perishing in very perilous circumstances, serve as eyes for the blind, pull sleds loaded with supplies across the frozen north, guard and protect property, locate and rescue lost and missing persons, bring livestock back to the barn each evening from pasture and put smiles on peoples faces on a daily basis all over the world.

This story is about an adorable, little dog with a big heart, called Sophie. She brings love and joy to everyone with whom she comes in contact. She is capable of softening the heart of the meanest, ugliest person alive.

Chapter 2

---•◦•———•———•◦•———

Brief History of
Bichon Frise

The Bichon Frise (pronounced, bee-chon free-zay), formerly the Bichon Teneriffe, came from the Canary Islands off the west coast of Africa. The breed received the name from the largest island in the group, Teneriffe and traveled all over Europe with Spanish and Italian sailors. The Bichon Frise; very beautiful to see, with a wonderful, white coat and black, lustrous eyes, has inspired many great painters; such as, Francisco Jose de Goya to include the Bichon Frise in their work. The breed became very popular in the 14th and 15th centuries with royalty and nobility in Italy, France and Spain. By the end of the 18th century, this playful little dog was befriended by an entirely different class of people.

The Bichon was often seen with Italian organ grinders and could even be found in circuses doing tricks. It is interesting to note that the Bichon did not come to the United States until 1955 and the first US-born litter occurred in 1956.

This breed of canine is often described as: feisty, playful, gentle, affectionate, sensitive with a small body and a big heart. The heroine of this story, Sophie, exemplifies all of these attributes.

Today, many prospective dog owners choose this particular breed of dog because they are suitable for folks with allergies; they are bred to be hypoallergenic. They supposedly do not shed or deposit allergens, such as, hair, dander and saliva on carpets and furnishings of the home.

Chapter 3

---•⊙•——•——•⊙•---

Polly Purchases a Dog

Sophie's owner and my best friend, Polly Pelletier tells the story of how the purchase of this amazing animal came about. Polly had relocated to Issaquah, WA from the state of Maine to escape from a bad marriage. Issaquah, WA is located 16 miles east of Seattle. She worked full time in a home based business with no social life. She very seldom left her dwelling; even going as far as purchasing groceries "on-line" with free home delivery.

At some point, Polly decided to buy a dog for companionship. She tried "on-line" again to locate the best breed of dog to satisfy her particular situation. The site which she visited required that she fill out a questionnaire designed specifically to match a new dog owner with the correct breed. Polly answered these questions to purposely paint a bad image of herself; as if she were lazy, selfish, obnoxious, impatient and just impossible to live with. The answer came back: Bichon Frise!

Polly thought, "Oh my God, that breed of dog would live with the Devil!" It soon became apparent, however, that this breed of dog was very expensive; between $2000 and $3000. She then decided maybe she could not afford a dog at that particular time. After a few more months of loneliness, she said to herself, "To Hell with it, I'm getting a dog!"

Realizing that her puppy was to be flown from British Columbia in Canada to Seattle, Washington at 3:00 o'clock in the morning, Polly packed a satchel full of items necessary to clean up the dog when she arrived. She was anticipating that the dog would have pooped and peed in the kennel in which she had been shipped. The people responsible for handing the puppy over to Polly in the receiving area, laughed at her, saying, "We don't carry that much stuff with us when we are traveling with our baby!" Sophie arrived prim and clean, waiting to do her business when the opportunity presented itself.

Upon departing from the terminal building, Polly tried to make her "potty" out of doors, but the dog refused to go because the entire area was covered with concrete. As soon as they got home and opened the door to the condominium, the dog went directly into the bathroom and used the litter box which had been prepared for her, exactly as she had been trained.

Sophie arrived at the airport in Seattle from a Canadian breeder, already litter box trained, at 12 weeks of age. She was born April 22, 2007. She is a cute, whiter-than-white, Bichon Frise with glamorous good looks and a charming personality. Her teddy bear looks, cuddly appearance and dark, expressive eyes make her a very easy animal to love.

When the new dog arrived at the airport, the customs agent asked, "What is your dog's name?" To which Polly answered, "Her name is Sophie!" Then he asked, "What's her middle name?" "She has no middle name," "Well, she has to have a middle name," insisted the agent. They finally settled on a middle name of Lauren. A new passport was issued for Sophie Lauren Pelletier. Yes, Sophie has a passport! She has also been registered with HomeAgain Microchip Identification System which is a protective recovery service that assists in locating a lost or stolen pet.

The breeder also required that Sophie be spayed; making her unable to be bred in the United States and ineligible to be shown in dog shows, as well. The rule being: an altered dog cannot be shown. This keeps the dog's pedigree safely in Canada!

Chapter 3x

Sophie Speaks Up

"OK, you guys, I get it! You want me to "pee and poo" in that funny looking box in the corner," I kept saying that to myself for weeks. By the time I was 12 weeks old, I was ready to move on with my life. Next, I found myself cowering in a small shipping crate aboard a jet airplane flying high in the sky between Canada and the United States. I was thinking, "Boy, I could really use that litter box now." Somehow I knew that I was enroute to new living quarters and a new master. "How long will this journey take," I thought, "Will I be able to hold out that long?"

Upon arrival at the airport in Seattle, the baggage handlers took me to meet a nice lady named, Polly (like the parrot) Pelletier, who was to become my new owner. It was love at first sight for both of us. She was pleasantly surprised to find me very neat and clean. You see, judging by the large tote bag full of cleaning materials that she was carrying, it was obvious that she was prepared to give me a bath, shampoo and grooming, if it became necessary, when I arrived.

At customs, there was a discussion over the way my name was to appear on the passport. My first name, Sophie, comes from the Greek, Sophia, which means: wisdom, skill. "I love it!" I'll bet most of my readers did not know that; well, I didn't know it either until I went on-line and Googled it. Most of the delay at customs was spent on choosing my middle name. The powers that be decided on Lauren. "Lauren, where did that come from?" I said to myself. Maybe it will never show up again, except on the passport. Oh, by the way, another thing I learned that didn't make me very happy; my Canadian breeders insisted that I be "fixed" so that I can never be bred and experience all the joys of motherhood. I can never be shown in a dog show either. All I can say, "What a bummer, I would have been a winner!"

When Polly and I left the terminal building, she gave me an opportunity to "potty" on the concrete and asphalt surfaces in the area. I absolutely refused to go there. It was just not my style. I looked up at Polly and my body language said, "No way, Jose. Not here!" As soon as we arrived home, however, and entered our apartment, I headed straight for the litter box in the bathroom which Polly had prepared for me and proceeded to relieve myself. "Now, that's my style!" She was very pleased and rewarded me with a treat and "mucho" special attention.

Polly had become very lonely prior to my arrival and we soon became very closely attached to one another; remaining close to the apartment and each other at all times. For about 4 years, between 2007 and 2011, we lived together in partial seclusion. We rarely went out into town except for visits to my vet and her doctor. In 2011, suffering from depression and loneliness, my owner, companion and best friend became very ill. She was not eating properly and was not communicating with her family and friends. Polly's daughter and son came to Issaquah to check on us. They found Polly lying unconscious on the living room floor and I was lying faithfully beside her keeping watch. After a visit to the doctor's, it was decided to bring my master and I back east to Dover NH, where we found a place to live and subsequently re-located. We packed up the things that we could carry and made the trip in Polly's car. It was a very long and unpleasant trip for me because, back then, I always got "car-sick." Thank God, that is no longer a problem for me. Polly ultimately got medical care and we moved into a first floor, studio apartment in Dover. There is a nice patio area here which is located conveniently for me to go outdoors to play and "potty." I have become somewhat of a celebrity here at Maple Suites. Everybody knows and loves me and I love everybody; the residents, staff and visitors. "Life is good here!"

Chapter 4

Sophie's Defining Attributes

There is no therapist in the world
as effective as a Bichon.

Sophie is a faithful companion and an excellent therapy dog. She goes everywhere with Polly and me. The only place we do not take her is to Mass (church) because she would surely disrupt the proceedings by diverting the attention of the congregation away from the priest. This little bundle of white fur is a huge hit when visiting nursing homes and rehabilitation centers. She is most popular with both patients and staff of these establishments; they all know her by name and recognize her each time she visits, even after a long absence. Upon entering the room of anyone that we have visited before and releasing her from the leash, she will jump on to the foot rest of their recliner right into their lap. Then, she often turns and smiles at the occupant of the recliner and begs with her expressive eyes to be petted.

On one occasion, when we were heading for the elevator to go home from the Rockingham County Nursing Home in Brentwood, NH. I heard a distorted voice say something which sounded like, "What a nice dog!" I turned and looked down the hallway and saw a crippled man in a specially equipped power chair. He looked and sounded like someone who had recently experienced a major stroke. I asked him if he would like to meet Sophie. He motioned to her and in a loud, clear voice, he shouted, "Yes!" I led the dog back to his chair and with a slight tug on her leash, she jumped right up into his lap. He hugged and cuddled her to himself as if she were a little baby. After a few minutes, he handed her back to me and said, in a distorted voice, "Thank you very much." Sophie had made his day, as well as all the by-standers who had witnessed the episode. The proud, little Bichon went prancing on down the aisle to the elevator, as if to say, "It's all in a day's work."

The Bichon Frise is very friendly; they rarely bark and seem to watch people closely. I can't imagine any other breed for a family.

Sophie is a people person. She loves everybody and everybody loves her. She does not do well with other animals. I am sure that this dog prefers humans to dogs. This is probably because she came from the breeder litter box trained and very seldom went out of doors. The first 4 years of her life were spent mostly indoors with no exposure to other animals.

Although the Bichon Frise is not widely considered to be one of the best watch dog breeds, Sophie is an outstanding watch dog. She is not big or aggressive enough to be a guard dog. She is, however, very territorial and possesses that extraordinary sense of smell required of watch dogs. With a low growl and a bark, she will make us aware of any strangers passing by our apartment door; even alerting us when we are away from home visiting people in nursing homes. When Sophie and I are hanging out in my apartment listening to music or watching TV, she will invariably look to the door a full 10 or 15 seconds before Polly comes through the door to join us. The dog picks up Polly's scent long before she arrives at my door. When another dog comes down the hallway, Sophie runs to the door and barks loudly until the strange animal gets well out of range of her "territory."

Sophie has a very charming smile. Yes, dogs do, indeed, smile! I remember one day, not long ago, a visitor to our retirement community was taking her picture, when the lady turned and remarked, "I think Sophie is smiling at me!"

I absolutely do not agree with those who say that "dogs do not actually smile." I cannot believe that when she is sitting down with two legs out in front of her, wagging her tail vigorously and apparently smiling with a broad "grin" on her face that she is actually preparing to bite me, as some people would have you believe. Sometimes, I swear she smiles as if she just told a very funny joke and is just waiting for me to get the punch line.

I once read in a book about Bichon Frise's; if you can keep your dog "smiling," you will be rewarded with unconditional love and playful times.

Sophie is so intelligent, she seems to be almost human. She is able to communicate with her body language; her eyes, tail, bark and movements, better than most humans do with speech.

That brings me to another issue I have been struggling over for a long time. Do dogs go to heaven? Does Sophie have a soul? Back in the 1930's, when I was a youngster, children were taught Catholic Christian Doctrine (CCD) from the old Baltimore Catechism. I was taught that animals do not go to heaven because they have no soul. Human beings have an intellect and a free will, therefore, they have a soul. That certainly suggests that our pets have no intellect or will. I have always disagreed with that idea.

Sophie has a greater intellect and a stronger will than most people I run into every day.

Has that doctrine changed? The short answer is: yes!

During a public audience in 1990, Pope John Paul II, the Holy Father, affirmed that animals, like men possess a soul. He said, "Animals too, have souls just like men." The Pope quoted several verses from Genesis of the Divine creative action of the Holy Spirit and also from Psalm 103 which states that there is no distinction between man and beast. This affirmation of the Pontiff raised enormous interest the world over and overjoyed thousands of Catholics. It also made pet owners very happy, confirming what they knew all along. We have all heard them say, "If my dog doesn't go to heaven, then I do not want to go either!"

Polly and Sophie can often be seen in a rocking chair in front of the building in which we live. They serve as unofficial greeters for everyone coming and going from the building. Visitors, residents, the mailman, movers, UPS persons, FedEx persons; everyone acknowledges the presence of this friendly, little white dog at the door. Sophie never disappoints these people; she rewards their attention with her good looks, charm and personality.

Sophie does very well with children because she is playful and has lots of energy. When first seeing her, they are immediately attracted to her with a strong desire to touch! When young children, accompanied by their parents, approach the dog in stores and shopping malls, I give the adult some kind of nod or sign to indicate that it's okay for the child to pet the dog. Actually, children from "1 to 92" cannot resist the desire to meet and pet this little, white powder-puff of a dog.

Sophie loves riding in a car! She enjoys riding up front on Polly's lap sitting in the passenger seat and listening to the music blaring from the on-board CD player with the 7 speaker sound around system. The dog has an uncanny ability to anticipate our arrival at the destination of each trip even though she may never have been there before. She gets prepared to leave the car before I shut the engine down. We recently took a 4 hour trip (each way) to Connecticut with Sophie aboard without incident.

Taking Sophie out of the house is like being with a celebrity. I am constantly stopped by people who want to pet her, enquire how old she is and comment on how beautiful and well behaved she is.

This precious, little dog also enjoys shopping and is usually welcome where ever we go. While walking through the stores and shops, we place her in the small basket part of the cart on a blanket, where she lies quietly taking in all the activity surrounding her. Interestingly enough, even when we enter places where pets are not normally allowed, the employees and customers become so entranced with her presence, they never ask us to leave. Sometimes, a manager or supervisor will approach us and say with a smile, "She's a service dog, right?" Polly and I nod and smile without saying a word and continue going about our business. In the checkout lines, the cashier and customers always make a big production over Sophie.

This incredible dog is most happy when all three of us are doing things together; that is, Polly, Sophie and I. Whenever the dog is alone with just one of us, she is constantly looking over her shoulder trying to locate the other. When Polly and I are sitting close together on the couch watching television, Sophie will usually jump up on the couch and snuggle down in the middle, forcing us apart. She then places her front legs on us; one leg on Polly and the other on me, to obtain our undivided attention.

Sophie does not particularly like going outside when it is raining, but she loves to romp and play in the snow. This can be a problem because she has a wonderful, white coat; it is very difficult to see her when it's snowing, especially at night.

The winter of 2014-15 produced record amounts of snow in the Dover, NH area and the snow was piled high all around the building in which we live.

One cold and snowy night, Polly put Sophie out to do "her business" in the patio area adjacent to her ground floor apartment. Because a great deal of snow had already fallen and drifted, creating a wall of snow about three feet high around the patio area, Polly did not attach the dog to the leash which was normally employed to keep her confined to the patio. When she went out of doors to retrieve her dog, Sophie was nowhere to be found. She was gone! Polly became alarmed and came running to my apartment, and bursting through the door, shouted, "Sophie is gone!" I dropped what I was doing and went to look for the dog.

Upon arriving at the spot where she was last seen, the snow was still falling and blowing around; the visibility was zero. I went out into the waist high snow looking for any trace of the missing dog; her tracks had already been covered up by the falling snow. After a few minutes of frustration, I came indoors, cold and wet and headed for the Manager's Office to report a missing dog.

As I walked by the Atrium, I saw Sophie sitting comfortably on a sofa there with three or four residents. The residents just smiled at me as if there was nothing wrong. I don't think that I have ever been more relieved in my life. I scooped the dog up and took her home to Polly. Later, I learned that after Sophie finished cavorting around in the blizzard, she found her way back to a lighted doorway located about 50 yards around the building from her own apartment; where she started to bark and scratch on the door with her claws. The people sitting in the Atrium opened the door and let her in. What I never did find out; is why they did not bring the dog back home or at least let us know she was all right. Everyone in the building knows the dog, to whom she belongs and where she lives. Did they suppose we let her out in a snow storm just to see if she could find her way home? That is how I know that Sophie is more intelligent than the average person.

Since Sophie had become a celebrity around our community, I thought it appropriate to place a name plate on the door of the apartment in which she resides along with Polly's. I thought, it must be colorful and it must be an attention getter. Being an amateur carver and woodworker, I came up with a design that looked like a marquee over the entrance of a movie theater. The placard is made of stained wood with the wooden letters "S-O-P-H-I-E" mounted symmetrically across it. Upon the letters, I cemented 53 tiny, colorful beads of red, blue, green, white and purple to simulate blinking "neon lights!" The sign is mounted with magnets to the metal hook which also holds the seasonal wreath or decoration that can usually be found on most apartment doors in the community.

Sophie has a quirk when it comes to accepting treats from total strangers. She absolutely will not take a treat offered by the man at the car wash or the receptionist at the veterinarian's office. These episodes remind me of when I was a child about to leave the house without adult supervision, my mother would say, "Don't take candy from strangers." Apparently, Sophie knows these things intuitively that we had to be taught, as children. Many people become upset with her when this dog refuses their offer. She will sometimes eat one of these treats if we take it home and offer it to her later. Her favorite is the Pup-Peroni Treat; the one that smells and tastes like pepperoni.

Another peculiarity of this dog occurs when she gets on and off the elevator in some of the nursing homes and rehabilitation centers which we enter on a daily basis. She performs a two legged, broad jump over the small opening that exists between the floor of the building and the elevator. It is such a quaint gesture that people in the area gather round to watch the performance. It is just one more of the cute mannerisms that identifies this little, white dog from all the rest.

The feisty animal makes the same grandiose leap every time she passes over the aluminum threshold located between the living room of my apartment and the outdoor patio. It is this kind of behavior that always brings a smile to my face and makes me so happy to have this little creature in my life.

Sophie thoroughly enjoys being groomed. She sits very quietly while being trimmed and brushed. She will voluntarily turn every which way to satisfy the groomers need to reach every inch of her body. This dog will even close her eyes, one at a time, to enable trimming the fur around them and cocks her chin from side to side which permits trimming under the chin. Sometimes, she becomes so relaxed that she actually closes her eyes and falls asleep during a grooming session.

Another of Sophie's hilarious diversions is when she wrestles with the "throw" pillows located on couches and recliners in the apartment. She stands on her hind legs and places her two front paws on the top of the pillow, where she pulls it down on the seat of the couch or chair.

Next, she lies flat on her back behind the pillow, and with both hind legs, kicks it off the couch onto the floor; growling and carrying on all the while. Then, the dog turns and "grins" at us with a tremendous sense of accomplishment! Sophie often goes through these gymnastics in my apartment while Polly and I are watching television. Sometimes she amuses herself in this manner when left alone in her own apartment for any length of time. Those are the times when we return to the apartment and find the pillows thrown everywhere. She has even been known to entertain everyone in the area this way, when we are visiting family and friends. There are moments, however, when the little bundle of fur simply hides behind the pillow and falls asleep instead of kicking it onto the floor. She loves to hang out behind or under a pillow, any kind of pillow.

Pillows are a large part of Sophie's life. One might even come upon her curled up and sleeping on one.

Chapter 4x

Sophie's Still Talking

"Yep, I am definitely a people person, or should I say, a people's dog. Hanging out with dogs or cats or any other kind of animal is not my cup of tea, you see?" The companionship and friendship of human beings is my strongest suit."

When Skip came into our lives, we became a family of three. We go everywhere together and do everything as a threesome. Now that I have overcome car sickness, riding in Skip's new Buick Lacrosse and listening to the music blaring from the seven speaker sound-around system is very cool! Visiting the sick and shut-ins has become a very rewarding experience for us, as well. I enjoy shopping, visiting, playing with children and just hanging out with my family.

Polly and I often sit together in front of our apartment building in a rocking chair serving as unofficial greeters to the people who are coming and going on a daily basis. These people always seem to remember me, fawning over me and making me feel very special. I always try to put my best foot forward so they are not disappointed.

If I remember correctly, that is how I got to really know Skip in the first place. He was walking laps around our building every morning after breakfast and each evening after supper in conjunction with his very successful weight reduction program. Polly and I counted his laps each time he passed by us encouraging and cheering him on. After his evening walk, Skip would join us to visit and chat into the night long after the doors of the building were locked for the day. I would pick up his scent as he approached long before any of us actually saw one another.

"Oh, man, it's pouring out there today." Everyone knows how I dislike going out in the rain. I wish I could walk between the falling drops. "Now, I am small, but not that small!" Take snow, on the other hand, I just love going out of doors when there is snow on the ground or even while the snow is actually falling. My white coat blends so well with the snow, I can barely be seen in a snow storm.

"Wow, that feels great!" I just lie back and relax while Skip trims and grooms me. As he brushes me, I twist and turn to present myself in each position as I anticipate his every move. "There, right there, that's it." He knows how I love to have my stomach brushed. I lie on my back with all four legs spread apart; my eyes closed while enjoying my special treatment. "See, I'm a good girl!" Skip is very good to

me; often cleaning my ears, clipping my toe nails and taking me to the vet.

A charming smile is one of my greatest assets. I have worked very hard to develop my warm and friendly smile which has been very rewarding and satisfying for me. Some people refuse to believe that dogs actually smile. "Shame on them."

Another of my favorite pastimes is to wrestle with throw pillows which can be found on rockers and couches in most apartments. At first, when I was a puppy, I would express my displeasure for being left alone for long periods of time, by tossing these pillows all around the apartment. Now, I enjoy spending my "alone time" by frolicking among the pillows wherever I find them.

Chapter 5

Medical Issues

Sophie suffers from Grand Mal seizures which is a form of epilepsy and is common among dogs of her type. She often experienced mild events as a puppy and Polly had been advised early on by the veterinarian that these were normal and not to be too concerned about them.

On March 22, 2015, however, Sophie was stricken with a very serious attack of seizures. It was on a Sunday afternoon, naturally, when all the veterinarian's offices are closed. Sophie and I were in my apartment waiting for Polly to return from shopping. Soon after Polly arrived, the dog began convulsions; shaking and running from room to room in a frenzy, bumping into walls and jamming herself into corners and frothing at the mouth. She was also urinating and defecating uncontrollably. It was very scary and frightening, coming about so suddenly!

At first, I did not know what to do; never having seen anything like this before. Polly was scared to death and began to cry out, "Oh, my God, we're going to have to put her down." I remember saying at the time, "Not so fast." Then I leapt into action. I knew that we had to get Sophie to a vet, pronto.

A few days earlier, while I was searching on my laptop for a new veterinarian, I came across an 800 number for emergency veterinary services in the state of New Hampshire. It had become necessary to locate a new vet because ours had suddenly shut down his office in Portsmouth and headed to the West Coast to care for his ailing father.

I am thinking: "What was that number? How can I find it now?"

My computer on the desk was "on-line": so I Googled "phone number for NH Emergency Veterinary Service." It popped right up and I dialed it on my cell phone. Then, I breathed a sigh of relief when a young, female voice said, "How may I help you?" I reported an 8 year old, female, Bichon dog experiencing severe seizures and asked, "What do I do?" The young lady on the other end of the line, asked, "How long has she been seizing?" Looking up at the clock on the wall for the first time since Polly had returned from shopping, I replied, "About 45 minutes." She said, "You must get that dog to an emergency clinic right away or she will suffer brain damage." "OK, tell me how to get where you are and we are on the way," was my reply. It turned out that she was in Concord, NH and we were in Dover; much too far apart to get the kind of attention we needed soon enough. The lady on the phone said she would find me an emergency veterinary clinic close by and ordered me to take Sophie's temperature in the mean time. Another warning that came over the phone: if the seizure lasts longer than 5 minutes, the dog is at risk of overheating; apply alcohol to her paws with cotton balls to cool her down. Handing the cell phone to Polly, I found a rectal thermometer and took the dog's temperature, doing exactly as I was directed. She was under my kitchen table shivering up against the wall making it very difficult to get near her. Her temperature was 108.6F, which I learned much later is not extremely high for a dog.

Returning to the phone, we exchanged information. After giving her Sophie's temperature, the lady gave me the phone number and approximate location of the Veterinary Emergency Care Center (VECC) in Newington, NH across the road from the entrance to the Fox Run Mall, about 15 minutes away. She advised me to call ahead to obtain specific directions to their location and to prepare them for the arrival of a seizing animal. She also suggested that we wrap the dog in a blanket and warned us to stay away from the dog's mouth and head to prevent the animal from biting us without knowing what she was doing.

I drove the car to the VECC while Polly held Sophie wrapped in a blanket in the passenger seat. On the way to the clinic, we looked at one another thinking, how would either of us have handled this situation if we had been alone. The dog stopped seizing and just looked dazedly at us with those dark, piercing eyes all the way to the emergency clinic. As soon as we arrived, Sophie started seizing again. We handed her over to a waiting staff of emergency care givers; who immediately prepared an IV site in each front leg, one for Valium and the other for a saline solution to keep her hydrated.

Upon completing the paper work at the registration desk, we were taken to a waiting room where we sat for about 2 hours wondering whether or not we got her there in time to prevent permanent damage to the dog's brain.

A female veterinarian finally came and told us that Sophie was stable and responding well to treatment. We were told that they were going to keep her over night for observation and laboratory work prior to prescribing long term medication. We had saved her life! We went home and waited for further instructions.

Later on, that same evening, when Polly and I were playing cards and listening to music in the Activities Room at Maple Suites, I received a call on my cell phone from the people at the VECC. They informed me that Sophie was doing well and that we should come in at 10:00 A.M. next morning to pick up a prescription for Phenobarbital, get it filled and return to the clinic so they could start her on a program to prevent future seizures. They also informed us that Sophie did not prefer to sleep in the kennel which they provide, but rather liked sleeping on a rug placed on the floor in front of her kennel.

The next morning, we filled the prescription and at around noon they started her on 12.6 mg of Phenobarbital taken orally, twice a day. Her IV's were removed and she was monitored for adverse side effects. Sophie was discharged later that afternoon and we took her home. After a thorough physical examination and lab work, the cause of the dog's seizure was never determined. For the record, the total cost of that emergency visit was over $1200. Dogs that take Phenobarbital require blood testing every 6 months because over time it can damage their liver. Sophie will probably require medication for the rest of her life. By trial and error, we learned that she will consume the tiny pill when it is placed in a small amount of peanut butter.

Sophie has experienced two more minor seizure events since being placed on medication. Both occurring between 3:00 and 4:00 A.M. and both lasting only a few minutes.

A few months after the major seizure event, Sophie began limping badly favoring her right front leg. I examined her very carefully attempting to find the cause of the limp, but could not find anything wrong. Two days later, she was hobbling around on 3 legs, keeping the right front leg off the ground. After taking her to the veterinarian in Somersworth, NH where Xrays were taken along with an examination, there was still very little evidence of what had caused the malfunction of that leg. The Vet prescribed two medications: Amoxicillin 25 mg, an antibiotic for infection and Carprofen 50 mg, a medication for Lyme disease, in the event the dog had been bitten by a tick, which had been reported active in the area at the time. After taking the medications for only two days, she began to walk and run around normally. We continued to administer the drugs for two weeks, as prescribed, and have noticed no ill-effects since then.

Chapter 5x

Sophie Wraps It Up

It was just another ordinary Sunday afternoon in March. Skip and I were hanging out watching sports on TV and Polly was out shopping. I distinctly remember when Polly came back and began showing us some of the items she had purchased.; probably between 1:30 and 3:00 PM.

The next thing I remember is being in a strange room with three or four people in white coats hovering over me. There was an IV site in each of my front legs and the room was spinning around. Some time later, one of the ladies in a white coat brought me to a small room where Polly and Skip were anxiously waiting to see me. Evidently, I had suffered a serious medical incident and was taken to an Emergency Clinic. It was then we all learned that they were going to keep me over night for observation and treatment.

"By the way, I didn't really like sleeping in that silly little box that they provided; so they let me sleep on a rug placed on the floor in front of it."

The following afternoon, after being discharged, I went home with Skip and Polly for good. It was great to get back into my own environment. However, soon I became aware that there was a little, white pill (Phenobarbital) hidden in peanut butter waiting for me twice a day, at meal times. "Looks like I will be taking this pill for the rest of my life."

One day, out of the blue, shortly after that incident, I began to limp very badly. My right, front leg began bothering me so much that I could no longer jump up on the couch or recliner. Skip examined me and could find nothing wrong with me. A couple of days later, that leg hurt so much that I could not put any pressure on it. I began hobbling around on three legs. Skip decided it was time to take me to a Vet, where Xrays and an intensive examination occurred. Still, there was very little evidence of what was happening with that leg. The Vet ultimately put me on two prescriptions and in a couple of days, just like magic, I was running and jumping normally again. "Man, I have no idea what those medications were called, but they surely worked well for me." I continued to take the meds, as prescribed, for two weeks and there has been no problem since. We are all very confused as to what really happened to me at that time.

"Guess what? Today is my birthday! (April 22nd) I am 9 years old. If I were a human person, I'd be 52 years old."

In order to determine that relationship, Skip and I did some serious research "on-line" at a Bichon Frise Information Station under the category: "Pet Years VS Equivalent Human Years"; which serves the worldwide Bichon Frise Community. "Actually, I don't feel a day over 40!" "I have never been more happy in my life, nor have I ever felt more healthy.

Chapter 6

Sophie's Longevity

I originally believed that 15 years would have been a very good life span for Sophie. But I since learned, that in 2004, a combined survey in the UK, USA and Canada determined the average life span of Bichon Frises to be about 12-13 years. The oldest dog of this breed, for which there are reliable records, is 19 years. Remember that people who live to be 100 years old are about the same as dogs who live to be 20. At the other end of the spectrum, a 3 year old canine is like a 21 year old human being.

Bichons are also prone to liver problems. Since Sophie is on Phenobarbital to control her seizures and that medication can damage a dog's liver, her longevity will be very difficult to predict. With all the love that Sophie gives and receives, I believe she will live a long time. Forget what they predict. Sophie is special!